Auto Focus

WOOD DETAILS

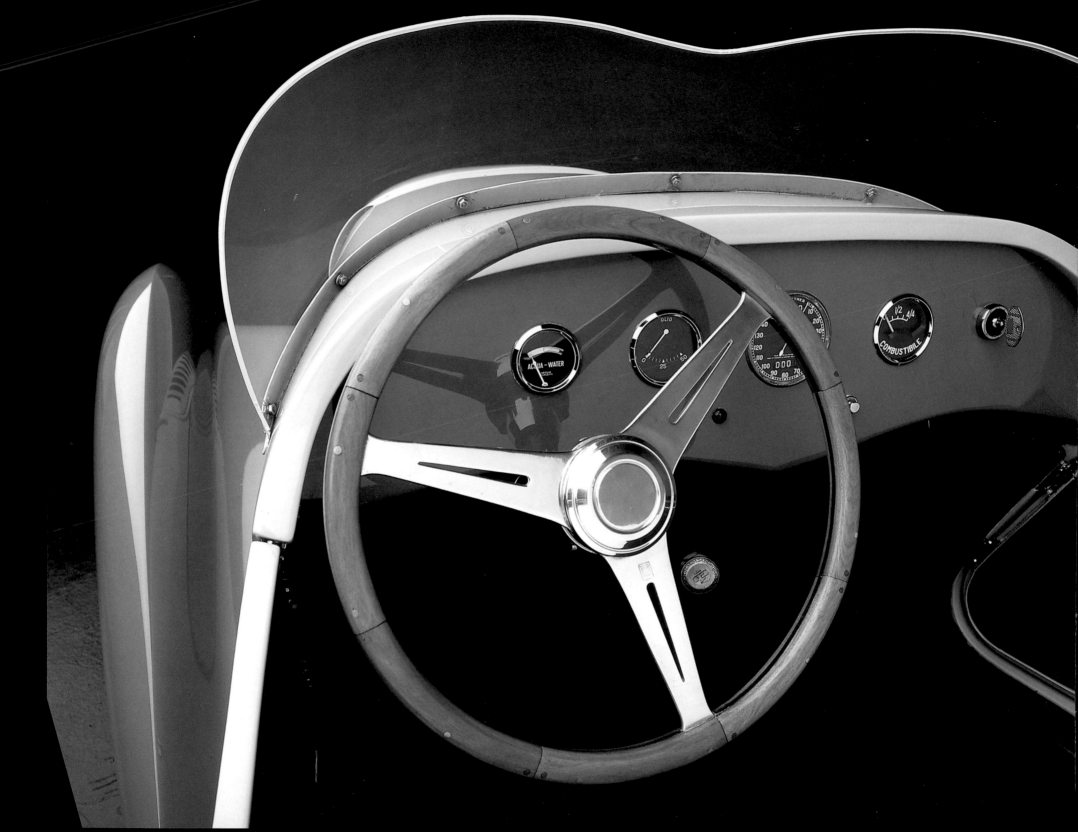

Auto Focus
WOOD DETAILS

Rob Leicester Wagner

FRIEDMAN/FAIRFAX
PUBLISHERS

A FRIEDMAN/FAIRFAX BOOK

Friedman/Fairfax Publishers
15 West 26th Street
New York, NY 10010
Telephone (212) 685-6610
Fax (212) 685-1307

Library of Congress Cataloging-in-Publication data available upon request

ISBN 1-56799-933-6

Editor: Ann Kirby
Art Director: Kevin Ullrich
Designer: Christina Grupico
Photography Editor: Wendy Missan
Production Manager: Camille Lee

Color separations by Spectrum Pte Ltd.
Printed in China by Leefung-Asco Printers Ltd.

1 3 5 7 9 10 8 6 4 2

Distributed by Sterling Publishing Co., Inc.
387 Park Avenue South
New York, NY 10016-8810
Orders and customer service: (800) 367-9692
Fax: (800) 542-7567
E-mail: custservice@sterlingpub.com
Website: www.sterlingpublishing.com
212/685-6610   FAX 212/685-1307

Contents

Introduction
From the Forest to the Dash

There's something about the look and feel of wood that brings warmth and ease to the senses. Even years after useful alternatives have become available, we still seek wood as a means to bring visual comfort when building furniture or decorating our homes. The deep, rich tones of mahogany, walnut, birch, oak, and cherry signify a quality unique in comparison to all other materials.

Wood had been the staple of automobile construction early on, a natural progression given that the auto's ancestry lies with horse-drawn buggies and the stately coaches of the nineteenth century. The introduction of the Pullman sleeper car further enhanced the use of wood furnishings in vehicles. By the end of the 1800s, train passengers could ride in luxury and comfort, surrounded by mahogany with inlaid mother-of-pearl or cherry wood. During the early years of the twentieth century, a majority of automobile bodies were paneled in wood.

Many of the turn-of-the-century vehicles were still paneled in wood. The British-made 1902 Arrol-Johnston typified the horseless-carriage style of the era with its fringed top and mahogany-paneled body. More elegant, but certainly radical for its time, was the custom-made wooden boattail 1914 Rolls-Royce Silver Ghost two-seater. American coachbuilders in particular, many of them holdovers from the horse and buggy days, depended on wood to decorate or to construct the frames of the

Above: **Packard made some of the most stunning wood-paneled cars ever mass produced.**
Opposite: **The burled walnut dashboard of a 1962 Rolls-Royce Silver Cloud, one of the British automaker's trademarks of elegant design.**

nation's automobiles. Brewster & Company of New York; LeBaron Carrossiers of New York; Brunn & Company of Buffalo; Willoughby & Company of Utica; Murphy of Pasadena, California; and Raymond H. Dietrich, who designed the most stately Lincolns ever, were considered the top coachbuilders in prewar America and Europe.

Automobile bodies from the turn of the twentieth century until World War II varied little. Wood, generally northern white ash, was used for the framework. Pieces were hand-cut and bent into shape with steam, or sanded to match the lines of the body. Coachbuilders usually set aside a large quantity of wood in the corner of a shop, allowing it to age for up to a year so that it would acclimate to room temperature and humidity. Wood framework was joined together with screws and glue, and wrought iron was employed to strengthen critical stress points or openings on doors and other moving parts. Occasionally cast bronze was used on the more expensive vehicles. Running boards were given the benefit of stronger woods, such as aged walnut or mahogany.

But carmakers soon found that wood could not accommodate new automotive designs, and advances in technology just before and shortly after World War I allowed aluminum, and later steel, to be shaped to provide the outer skins for automobiles. But wood remained as a decorative device for coachbuilders of such luxury marques as Cadillac, Packard, Isotta-Fraschini, Delage, and Hispano-Suiza. Applications of wood for aesthetic rather than practical purposes ranged from a subtle touch of mahogany on the running boards of the Isotta-Fraschini Tipo 8A Dual Cowl Phaeton to the excess of the Hispano-Suiza Type 68 V12, which was paneled from radiator to rear in tulip wood and fastened by rivets.

While the Hispano-Suiza was indeed a beauty, a car paneled in wood was hardly practical, and had little to recommend it in terms of performance. Such cars, especially less expensive ones, creaked and groaned. Rain and heat wreaked havoc as wood expanded and shrank with the changing seasons. Only loving attention to varnishing—a high-maintenance job, to put it mildly—could keep a wood-bodied vehicle from looking like a sorry mess after just a few years on the road.

Yet despite its shortcomings wood thrived, as carmakers continued to incorporate splashes of wooden trim into their designs. By the mid-1920s, subtle use of wood trim was commonplace. Walnut became the favored wood for interior details, especially among European coachbuilders, who used the dark hardwood for window trim, division housing, vanities and refreshment cabinets, small tables, and toolboxes mounted on the running boards, usually complemented by the finest leather for the seats or silk-covered upholstery. European sports car makers continued the trend: Jaguar traditionally uses burled walnut on its dashboards, and Aston Martin also favored walnut dashes for many of its prewar cars. Delage used burled walnut and oak conservatively during the 1920s, with eye-popping results—its DI Series 1926 model, a dual-cowl workhouse for the automaker, had its door trim and cowl in front of the rear passenger compartment crafted in walnut. Its boat-style boot was also covered on top in walnut trim. In chauffeur-driven limousines, passenger interiors were often paneled in mahogany with a satin

veneer inlaid with mother-of-pearl. The truly ambitious often used solid gold or silver for interior fittings, such as door handles or locks.

Yet the love of wood went far beyond the luxury market. Even as advances in the use of aluminum and sheet metal prompted automobile designers to evolve rapidly through the years (consider that styling progressed from horse and buggy through the Edwardian era to the influences of the French-made Renaults and to Art Deco and Industrial design in the span of about forty years), stylists couldn't resist returning to wood-paneled designs to accent body images. Heavy emphasis on exterior wood paneling—as steel and aluminum became commonplace—began not with luxury cars, but with the granddaddy of the station wagon and the legendary postwar woodie, the depot hack.

The depot hack was a common sight in the early part of the century, ferrying train passengers from train depots

to hotels in town. The first wood-bodied depot hack, the Star, appeared in 1923 and was the brainchild of former General Motors chief Billy Durant. But it was Henry Ford who seized on the idea and mass produced the wood-bodied commercial vehicle. In 1929, Ford produced nearly 5,000 Model A station wagons, the first of the legendary woodies sung about by such surfer bands as the Beach Boys and Jan and Dean some twenty-five years later. Other manufacturers followed Ford's lead, creating a niche market for utilitarian but stylish vehicles, always accented with a bit of wood paneling.

In our current era of practicality, wood is once again a detail reserved for the very wealthy. Restored vintage woodies are among the most desirable—and expensive—of all classic cars. And on the new car market, automakers from Jaguar to Toyota still look to walnut, oak, and mahogany to give their higher-priced automobiles a touch of élan.

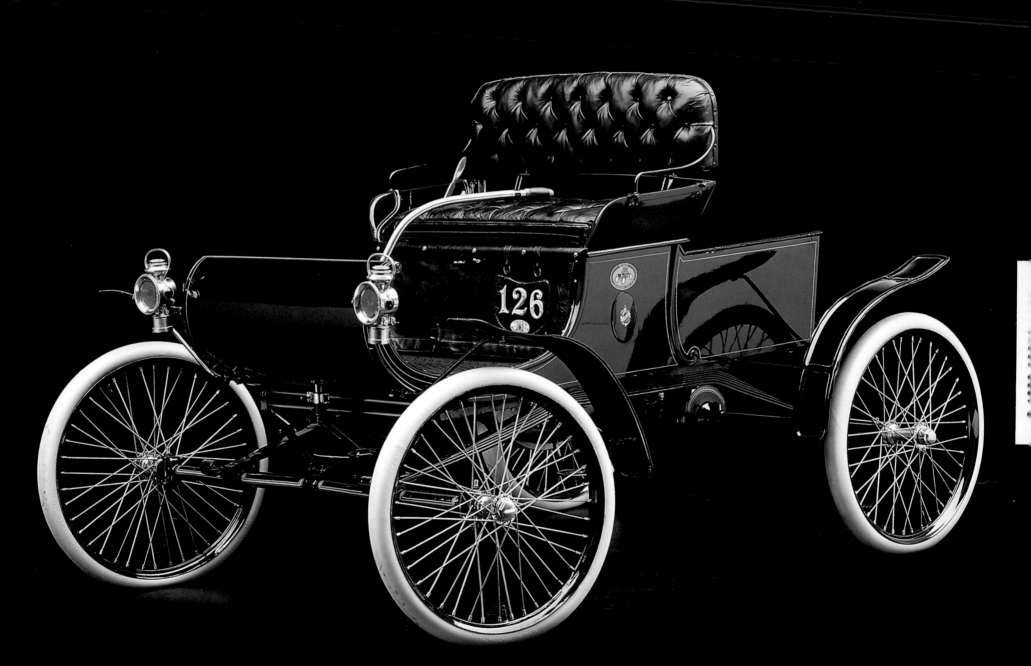

From Coach to Car
Traveling Through the Gilded Age

One hundred and fifty years ago, long-distance travel was a grueling, time-consuming, often nasty experience. Traveling for a week by rail from New York to San Francisco meant sitting on hard, wooden benches and eating cold, greasy food. Journeying by ocean liner could be just as miserable. Being uncomfortable during lengthy trips in the mid-nineteenth century was an accepted part of life.

By the 1880s and '90s, travel by rail changed dramatically with the introduction of the sleeper car. There was little luxury, but the fact that one could sleep in a bed and have a sense of privacy now made train travel a relatively comfortable experience. Sleeper cars evolved much like other modes of transportation, and soon small touches would be added to provide comfort and a sense of style for the traveler. The very wealthy soon found that customized personal sleeper cars provided them not only privacy and protection from the riffraff in other cars, but all the comforts and luxury of home as well.

This theme soon made its way to ocean travel, as luxury liners built just after the turn of the century began to cater to the tastes and expectations of the well-to-do on two continents. First-class staterooms were paneled in oak and mahogany, thickly carpeted, and furnished with silk-covered chairs and divans, giving passengers all the comforts of a moving mansion.

But even in this Gilded Age, coachbuilders did not immediately marry comfort and luxury to the automobile.

Opposite: **The revolutionary 1901 Oldsmobile runabout with curved dashboard. The curved dash concept was born from the ashes of a factory fire by Oldsmobile founder Ransom E. Olds.**

Above: **The pressure gauges, executed in brass, looked stunning against the hardwood dash in the 1907 Rolls Royce 40/50 Silver Ghost.**

The automobile during the first decade of the twentieth century was, in fact, truly a horseless carriage, hardly more than a self-propelled open carriage providing little or no protection from the weather and only a modicum of cushioning on the seats. To the coachbuilder, and for that matter to many men and women of the era, the automobile was merely a hobby for the wealthy, rather than a refined—or even practical—means of transportation.

Perhaps the first seeds of automotive design, and ultimately the coupling of coachwork and engineering, didn't come from the master coachbuilders of New York and Europe but from a Michigan entrepreneur. Ransom Eli Olds had been tinkering with the automobile since 1887, first with a rather impractical three-wheeled steamer and later with a gasoline-powered car. In 1899, his Olds Motor Works began producing experimental Oldsmobiles. A fire burned down the Detroit factory in 1901, but a single gasoline-powered vehicle was rescued: the wood-bodied curved dash runabout that was steered with a tiller. This vehicle had a little something that other early automobiles of the day lacked: panache.

The White company, which later would become famous for is sturdy truck line, also made liberal use of wood in its early car models. Its 1911 steamers, which would see service as one of the official presidential cars during the Taft administration, featured carefully wood-crafted dashboards and flooring with a substantial set of gauges that appeared decidedly nautical.

From Coach to Car

When the construction of the automobile became less dependent on wood, luxury car makers still preferred to use wood in great quantities for aesthetic reasons. Customers of Rolls-Royce and Bentley, in particular, often had coachbuilders elaborately panel their interiors, and occasionally the exteriors, in wood.

The use of cherry and mahogany woods to execute elaborate designs, ranging from hand-carved figures and designs to inlaid mother-of-pearl had become de rigueur among New York coachbuilders as a way to distinguish the standard luxury car from the true high-end ultra luxury vehicle.

Below: **The wood-spoked wheels of a 1909 White M steamer, an early pioneer in wood-framed automobiles.**

Right: **Coachbuilders such as Brewster, LeBaron, J. Rothschild & Fils, and others executed elaborate interior wood paneling, as in this 1927 Rolls-Royce Phantom I. This example of Victorian-flavored automotive design was performed by Brewster of New York.**

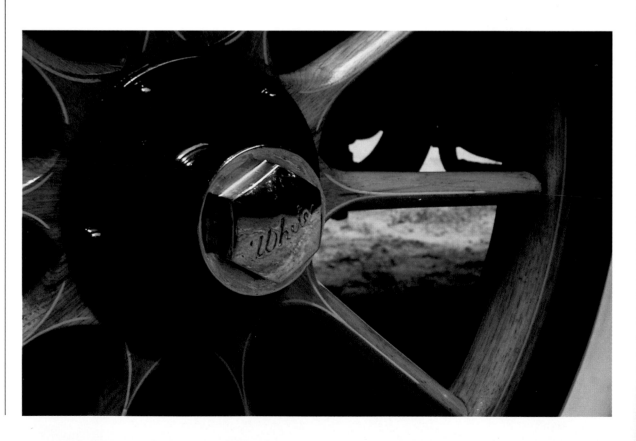

A fine skiff of early post–World War I vintage. The absence of heavy metal work and running boards saved considerable weight.

15

Left: This 1903 curved dash Oldsmobile runabout was powered by a three-horsepower engine and steered with a tiller.

Opposite: A 1914 Rolls-Royce Silver Ghost skiff. Although this version employs doors, many skiffs were built without them to ensure rigidity. Note the canvas top and spare tire cover, which complement the wood motif.

Above: **A Spartan but nonetheless
complete set of gauges for a 1907
40/50 Rolls-Royce Silver Ghost.**

Opposite: **A 1903 Mercedes
60-horsepower two-seater
that employs wood for visual
appreciation rather than framing.**

Left: The distinctive wheel hub of
an early Rolls-Royce.

Below: Flooring and dashboards
were commonly constructed of
mahogany by coachbuilders
of the Edwardian era.

Opposite: Brewster coachbuilders
were known worldwide for elaborate
and intricate use of wood paneling
on luxury cars, in this case a 1930
P1 Town convertible.

21

Left: Jump seats on a 1914 Rolls-Royce Silver Ghost skiff.

Opposite: Nineteenth-century horseless carriages were almost entirely constructed of wood, as illustrated by this three-wheeled model with a tiller.

Pages 24–25: Rolls-Royce has always been on the cutting edge of luxury and styling, as the refined touches of wood on this 1907 40/50 Silver Ghost model attest.

Natural Luxury
Automotive Evolution

With technology improving following World War I and most coachbuilders of the day focusing on using wood for its aesthetic qualities, some automakers saw wood as a way to enhance performance, both to reduce weight and to increase aerodynamics.

One such coachbuilder was Jean Henri-Labourdette, a visionary and prolific French stylist, who was challenged in 1912 to come up with a "nautical" aerodynamic design for an automobile that could be competitive in racing. The result was the forerunner to the classic sports cars of the 1930s and '40s. While the prewar and postwar Aston Martin, Alfa Romeo, and Mercedes-Benz did not employ wood in their body styling, they owe at least a nod of gratitude to Labourdette for his adherence to lightweight construction and designs that significantly reduced wind resistance.

In 1912, French racing legend Rene de Knyff commissioned Labourdette to build an ultra-light closed body automobile. Following the success of Labourdette's first design effort, de Knyff challenged the stylist to come up with a comfortable "torpedo" that provided little wind resistance. Labourdette soon constructed a skiff that employed triple layers of mahogany planking riveted to an ash wood frame. The car, to become known as the "Skiff de Knyff," was styled in a manner unheard of in coachbuilding circles; cars of the day—and in fact through the early 1930s—were constructed on a chassis with an

Opposite: **Very few skiffs or boattails survive today; this 1924 Rolls-Royce Silver Ghost Boattail Speedster is extremely rare.**

Above: **Wood veneer was used on the wheels and suspension system of this 1926 3-liter Bentley. Body work on this long chassis version was executed by Barker coachbuilders.**

engine, hood, and cowl. Labourdette, on the other hand, constructed a hood that sloped upward to the cowl with the rear portion of the vehicle continuing the trend that ended in a point at the rear. It was a graceful form, considered revolutionary for its time. And, owing to Labourdette's appreciation of the natural beauty of wood, the mahogany was left in its natural state

Competing coachbuilding firms also appreciated Labourdette's accomplishments, and instituted their own designs. LeBaron, Rothschild, Barker, Holbrook, Lavocat & Marsaud, and Million-Guiet all at one time produced their own versions of the Labourdette skiff. Some coachbuilders used mahogany and others wood veneer. Barker coachbuilders used wood veneer on its wheel covers and exposed front suspension system on Bentleys, most notably the 1926 3-liter long chassis model. Other stylists preferred a lightweight aluminum instead of wood.

Rolls-Royce vehicles were a natural for skiff construction. Examples include a 1930 Phantom II that is virtually all wood from the cowl rearward except for the fenders and running board; the 1937 25/30 dual cowl skiff that employed a ribbed natural finish on its pointed boot area; an extremely rare example of a 1921 model that has a distinctive pre–Art Deco motif; and a two-seater 1924 Silver Ghost Boattail Speedster. Barker used wood extensively on a 1926 Rolls-Royce 20-horsepower cabriolet de ville. Not only had the body, fenders, and running boards been paneled in wood, but the interior was well-appointed in a wood motif, including the dashboard, door trim, and even hand brake.

Few examples of Labourdette's work have survived, but his legacy has endured through the decades. Conservative customers may not have embraced the radical designs of Labourdette, but the seduction of wood-grained body paneling could not be denied.

Right: The wood steering wheel gives this 1929 Bugatti Type 41 Royale a sense of comfort and high styling.

Opposite: Wire wheels and motorcycle-type fenders covered in mahogany veneer provide a striking contrast to the ash wood deck on this prewar skiff.

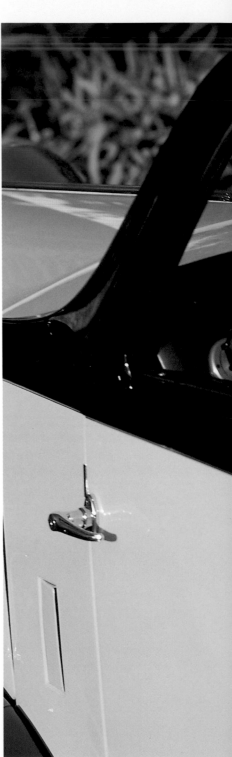

Above: Flawless paint, gleaming chrome, and glowing hardwoods are a stunning combination, as evidenced by the running boards on this 1933 Isotta Fraschini.

Right: Deep, rich tones of walnut warm the interior of this pristine Type 50 T Bugatti. Chrome hardware gleams on both the driver and passenger side of the hardwood dash.

Above: Jaguar usually paneled its
dashboards in burled walnut. This
model is a 1951 3.5-liter MK V.

Opposite: Radical skiff design with
motorcycle-type fender treatment
and canvas top make this stately
1930 Rolls-Royce Phantom II
Boattail very daring.

Left: Wood-paneled dashboard and leather-trimmed doors provide the perfect detailing for this 1923 Bentley three-liter short chassis tourer.

Opposite: Buick often employed liberal wood construction in the years before World War I. This is a 1912 tourer powered by a 22.5-horsepower engine.

Pages 36–37: Buicks—conservatively styled cars aimed at middle- and upper-middle class Americans—still offered wood trimming as late as 1928. While many cars of the era employed steel wheels, this 1928 roadster continued to roll on wooden spokes.

Opposite: Elaborate instrument panel of a 1954 Jaguar XK120 drophead coupe, an early version of the famous XK series created by the British automaker.

Right: Barker coachbuilders produced this wood-bodied 1926 Rolls-Royce 20-horsepower cabriolet de ville. By any standard, this kind of wood-bodied vehicle would be difficult to maintain.

Opposite: A 1907 Rolls-Royce
40/50 Silver Ghost Roi de Belges
by J. Rothschild & Fils.

Right: The rear end of
a 1926 Rolls Royce by
Barker coachbuilders.

Right: The no-nonsense and easy-to-read dashboard of a 1938 dark blue Bugatti Type 57SC.

Opposite: By the late 1930s the so-called skiff design had gone out of fashion. But Rolls-Royce owners still enjoyed toying with the styling. Here is a rare combination of Art Deco and skiff design on a 1921 Rolls.

Style and Speed
Cruising on Land

Jean Henri-Labourdette's radical use of mahogany as a weight-saving device was never fully embraced by many automakers. Technology had advanced by the 1920s to allow builders to focus on aluminum as the preferred choice of construction.

While race car builders eschewed the luxury trappings of wood-grained paneling on the exterior and interior of their vehicles, the same cars they were racing had to be sold to the public. Marques like Alfa Romeo, Aston Martin, and Delage were serious contenders on the racetrack, but they were also sold to the general public. What wood-grained dashboards and door trim were to the average country driver, engineering and engine performance were to the race driver; to sell the car in sufficient quantities, these elements had to be combined.

Aston Martin favored light treatment of wood on its cars. In 1932, the Le Mans, named after the famed French endurance race, debuted. Although not particularly aerodynamic, the Le Mans featured a boattail rear, echoing treatments already used by other automakers. Sleekly designed with motorcycle fenders, external exhaust, and a forest green body, the little roadster was accented with a walnut dash and steering wheel.

Racing Bentleys rarely, if ever, displayed external wood bodies or trim, but its dashboards and door trim often featured cherry wood or walnut styling to cluster a wide array of gauges. The "Red Label" three-liter series, produced between 1921 and 1927, made liberal use of

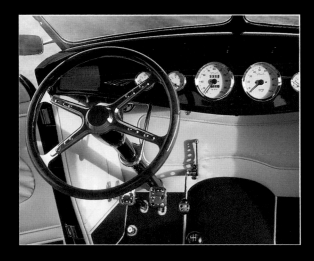

Opposite: **The legendary tulip wood 1933 Hispano-Suiza Type 68 V-12 was actually driven in endurance races, but its wood-constructed body didn't fare well.**

Above: **The polished wood steering wheel and dash of a 1932 Ford Roadster.**

these elements for the public. While interior wood trim could be found on racing versions of the Bentley, the styling was primarily reserved for the general public.

Wood-bodied American cars debuted shortly before the United States' entry into World War II, but their popularity surged after the war with wood bodies applied to convertibles, hardtops, and the family station wagon. With the Depression a memory and a newly stimulated economy, Detroit was ready for the fanciful and eager to celebrate its new prosperity.

Chrysler had debuted its elaborate wood-bodied cars in late 1941 with the Town & Country two-door convertible, the four-door sedan, and its high-end New Yorker. For the 1946 model year, the first year of automobile production after the war, the Town & Country returned with its prewar styling. The heavy wood-bodied Town & Country convertible had its entire trunk paneled in ash. The New Yorker could be ordered with a wood-framed roof luggage rack complete with ribbing to protect the roof.

Ford's answer to Chrysler was its similar Sportsman model, available on either a Ford or Mercury chassis. The Sportsman was attractive, with its coordinated wood-grained walnut dashboard to match the ranch-style exterior design consisting of finger-joined ash framing. Hand-crafted wood, harvested from Ford's own forest in Michigan, quickly became the Sportsman's hallmark. All wood pieces were cut from solid blocks; there was no shaping from steam. Finger joints provided sturdy construction, but the pieces were so carefully installed that seams were impossible to detect by touch.

Detroit's experimentation with wood-bodied vehicles didn't last, but it illustrates car manufacturers' curiosity—perhaps nostalgia—with regard to vehicles that exuded warmth and a general comfort level not often found in postwar offerings. For the most part, American automakers were shy in their efforts to incorporate wood designs into cars, leaving European sports car and luxury car manufacturers to indulge without much competition from Detroit.

The classic styling of running boards, wire wheels, and walnut dashboard made the T-series MG perhaps the most popular postwar British sports car in the United States.

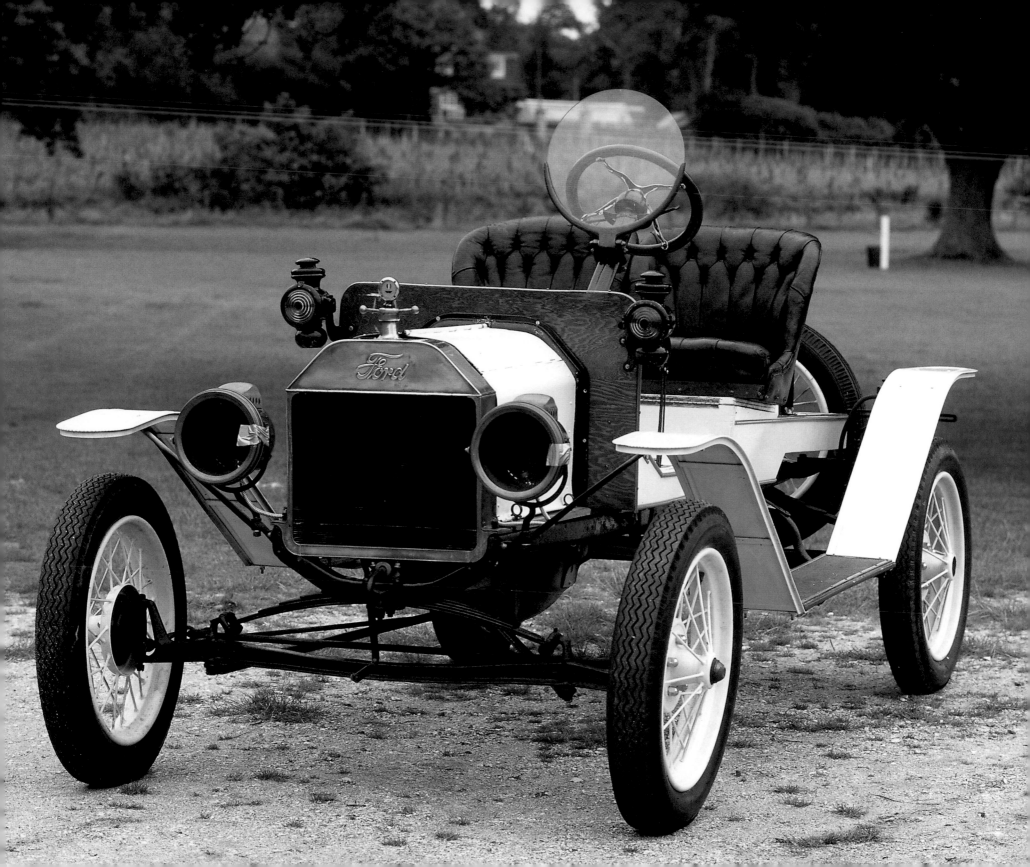

Opposite: The 1914 Ford Model T roadster showed little change from the original Model T, which debuted in 1908. Much of its construction derived from ash wood framing.

Right: The 1932 Aston Martin LeMans two-seater was designed and styled for racing, and proved to be quite successful on the track. It was then put on the market for the motoring public.

Pages 50–51: The 1911 Mercer was
one of the fastest cars on the race
circuit in the United States. Even
the legendary Stutz had difficulty
unseating the Mercer from its
perch as the top race performer.

Above: The wood framing of the
flooring and dashboard area of
a pre–World War I vintage auto,
the 1906 Fiat.

Right: A 1906 Fiat 28/40 Targa
Florio type 7.36-liter model.

Pages 54–55: The 1948 Chrysler Town & Country convertible came to typify the stately living of the upper middle class and the wealthy in postwar United States.

Left: Almost since the inception of the automobile at the turn of the twentieth century, automakers were fascinated with the use of woodgrain for dashboards as an aesthetically pleasing element to automotive design.

Above: A 1937 MG. Little changed from model year to model year among the MG T Series cars.

Opposite: **The 1947 Ford Model 71 Sportsman convertible became popular immediately after World War II, but its high-maintenance wood paneling doomed sales.**

Below: **Craftsmanship is the name of the game when constructing wood paneling for the exterior of a car. Each piece must be seamlessly joined to its neighbor, with the joints undetectable by touch.**

Right: **Wood interior paneling and leather trim subtly complement the exterior of this Chrysler.**

Right: A customized 1932 Ford roadster is highlighted by a solid wood steering wheel.

Opposite: The Chrysler Town & Country four-door sedan was beautifully crafted in mahogany and ash wood framing.

60

Pages 62–63: Sales of the
1948 Chrysler Town & Country
wood-paneled four-door sedan
numbered 3,994, making that year
one of the automaker's best for
sales of the ranch-style car.

Left: Not particularly known for its
wood-framed styling, Chevrolet
nonetheless came up with some
fine, if restrained, examples
of woodie styling. This is
a 1947 Fleetmaster.

Above: As with fine furniture,
the beauty of wood-framed
construction is in the details.

Opposite: Weighing in at 3,957
pounds, the 1948 Chrysler Town &
Country was easily the heaviest
family sedan in the Chrysler line.

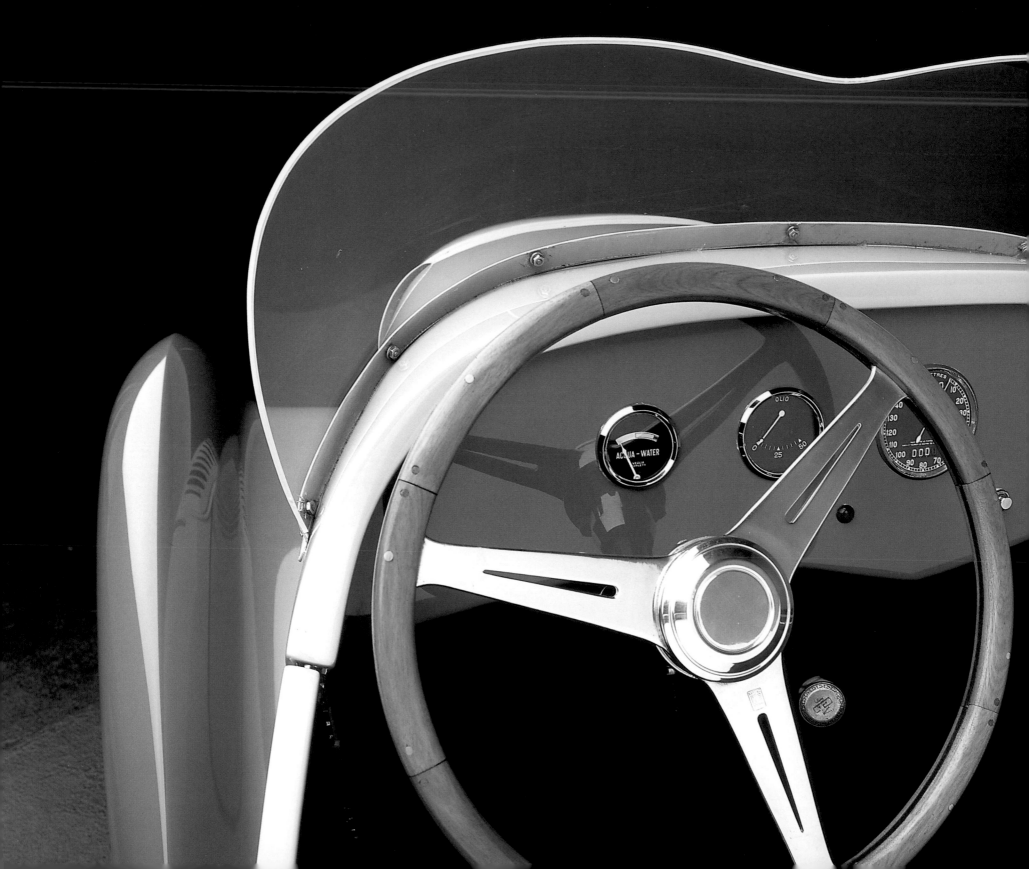

Right: The stark racing lines of the dashboard of this 1938 Siata Zagato starkly contrast, yet perfectly complement, the natural wood steering wheel.

Left: Strictly no-nonsense is the spartan interior of this Delage.

69

Chapter Four

Classic Woodies
The First Sport Utility Vehicles

Notwithstanding the attractive and functional European nautical-styled skiffs, wood-bodied vehicles can trace their roots to the depot hacks of the early 1920s. Billy Durant, General Motors' former president, initiated the use of wood-bodied vehicles for commercial transportation of both passengers and goods with the Star depot hack.

But it was once again Henry Ford who had the ability and the foresight to take a good idea and mass produce it. His 1929 Model A quickly became the sport utility of its day: big, stylish, and practical, it was as at home performing heavy-duty chores on Kansas farms as it was moving stars and moguls about the back lots of Hollywood. Ford would dominate the market throughout the next several decades, offering not only the classic Model A, but more luxurious variations on the theme from the automakers' more upscale Mercury marque.

In the years following World War II, the Ford wagon continued to rule the woodie roost. Between 1949 and 1951, Ford produced some of the most attractive woodies, including the legendary shoebox woodies, with wooden outer panels covering a strong all-steel frame.

Other marques offered wood-bodied wagons of their own. Despite GM's pioneering of the depot hack, the company was relatively late in the game on the mass market, introducing its first woodie in 1937 with the Pontiac Quality Six Station Wagon. Buick offered a woodie in its station wagon line that included on some models a simple

Opposite: **The granddaddy of all woodie wagons is this 1922 Star depot hack, originally conceived to move passengers and goods from train depots into town. It was the brainchild of former General Motors head Billy Durant.**

Above: **Note the virtually seamless construction of this woodie.**

ash framing and mahogany along its windowsills and door trim, leaving the body panels exposed. Its interiors, on both prewar and postwar models, were trimmed in wood with a mahogany veneer dashboard. Plymouth's offerings dated back to the late 1930s, with an all-ash wood framing and body paneling to the more interesting mahogany paneling and ash frame versions found on the later postwar models.

Perhaps the most unusual line of woodies, and certainly the most sought after by collectors, were luxury woodie wagons. Cadillac produced a hybrid in 1941. It was a two-door fastback model sheathed in mahogany and framed in ash with matching luggage rack. Packard also produced some fine examples of wood-bodied cars. Its 1941 110 line was a custom-bodied station wagon fitted with an ash framing with either maple or mahogany paneling, and interior door trim of ash.

By 1951 it had become apparent to automakers that constructing woodies was an expensive task with little return on investment. Resales of woodies were poor: without continued and attentive care, the wood quickly deteriorated, and buyers of new cars complained to dealers of the condition of their wood-paneled cars within a year or two of purchase. The surfers of the era—who appreciated the board-friendly luggage racks and spacious interiors—reaped the benefits of the woodie's troublesome nature: rusted and rotted "termite trucks" could be purchased for as little as seventy-five dollars, and the warm, dry climate of southern California was kind to the cars' temperamental foundations.

By the mid-fifties, the Big Three had begun phasing out production of wood-paneled wagons and cars. But at the same time, they began producing a lesser version of the wood-bodied car, turning out station wagons that featured a wood veneer glued to metal body panels and framed in ash. It was a cheap substitute, but managed to sell well enough. Buyers, it seemed, still craved that bit of wood trim, and were willing to take what they could get.

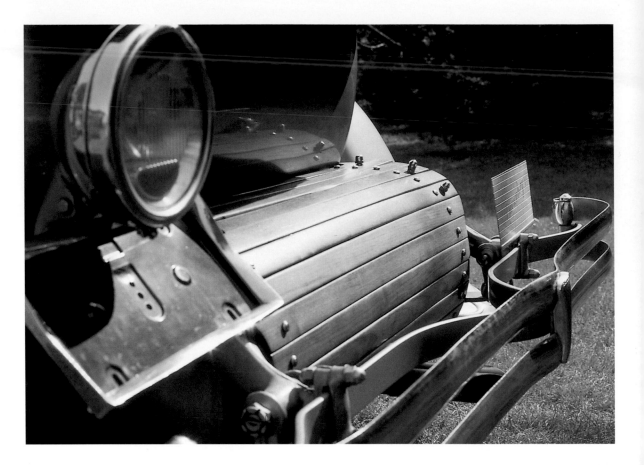

Above: **Murphy coachbuilders added these wood touches to a 1930 Duesenburg.**

Opposite: **This 1899 Benz "Dos à Dos," constructed almost entirely of wood, typified the boxy, crude development of body styling during the early years of automotive history.**

Henry Ford capitalized on
Billy Durant's idea of a woodie
wagon by mass-producing his own
version in the late 1920s. His 1929
Model A was a tremendous sales
success, and this woodie version
sold well in rural areas, especially
to the wealthy ranchers and
gentlemen farmers.

Left: Before there was the Star and before Henry Ford's ranch wagons debuted, there was the Napier. This version is a 1913 estate wagon powered by a 16-horsepower engine. These models were often found performing workhorse duties throughout Europe.

Below: The simple but elegant construction of the dashboard and flooring of this 1908 Mercedes tourer was standard styling for the German automaker in the years before the First World War.

Opposite: **Several layers of varnish
protect the wood ash framing
of this 1940 Packard 1801
station sedan.**

Right: **The fittings of a 1949–50
Chrysler Royal. Once a utilitarian
alternative to the Town &
Country, restored Royals
are among today's most prized
collector woodies.**

Pages 80–81: Ford's "shoebox" woodies of 1949–51 were among the most popular woodies ever, as returning GIs snapped up the pretty two-door wagons and headed for the suburbs. Nonetheless, Ford would move to all-steel construction for 1952.

Left: Chromed rivets complement the ash frame and mahogany paneling of this classic woodie.

Right: A large clock nestles neatly in the dashboard of a 1948 Ford woodie.

Pages 84–85: A very rare 1941 Cadillac custom wood-paneled two-door estate wagon. Note the industrial design, influenced by the Art Deco styling of the previous decade.

Opposite: Only 1,746 two-door Mercury wagons were produced for the 1949 model year, and just a fraction of those were woodies. These high-end cars from Ford are very rare today and command top prices among collectors.

Right: Utilitarian interior of a 1941 Packard woodie.

Above: **By the early 1950s, Ford had given up on wood-bodied cars, arguing that they were too costly to produce and too difficult for the buyer to maintain. But the automaker continued to offer wood-themed styles for diehard enthusiasts, as with this 1956 Country Squire, paneled in simulated woodgrain.**

Right: **Sturdy vertical posts supported the roof and doors on the woodies of the 1930s.**

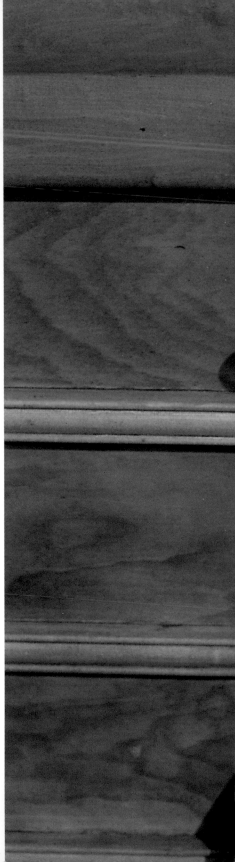

Opposite: Only 555 Plymouth
Suburbans were produced in 1938,
the first year for the wagon.

Pages 92–93: By 1949, the use of
wood was declining in American
cars. Plymouth continued to offer
its woodie wagon, like this 1950
model, but an all-steel version
was offered as well.

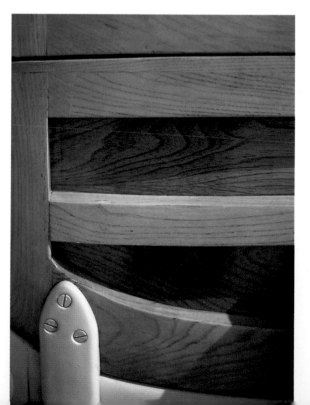

Above: The commodious interior
of a 1941 Buick woodie.

Right: Most woodies used a
two-piece tailgoate design, with
upper and lower components.
Easy access to ample storage made
these cars especially appealing to
the surfers of the next generation.

Suggested Reading

Automobile Quarterly, Vol. 23, No. 2. (April 1985).

Automobile Quarterly. Vol. 34, No. 2 (July 1995).

Carson, Richard Burns. *The Olympian Cars.* New York: Alfred A. Knopf, 1976

Gunnell, John A. (ed.). *Standard Catalog of American Cars, 1946–1975.* Iola, Wis.: Krause Publications,1982.

Halberstadt, Hans. *Woodies.* New York: Metrobooks, 2000.

Kimes, Beverly Rae (ed.). *Standard Catalog of American Cars, 1805–1942.* Iola, Wis.: Krause Publications, 1989.

Narus, Donald J. *Chrysler's Wonderful Woodie: The Town & Country*, Parma, Ohio: Venture Publishing, 1988.

Sedgwick, Michael. *Cars of the Thirties and Forties.* New York: Beekman House,1979.

Wagner, Rob L. *Classic Cars*. New York: Metrobooks, 1996.

Photo Credits